# TALKING ABOUT MYSELF

# DEPRESSION

Interviews by Angela Neustatter
Photographs by Laurence Cendrowicz

W

FRANKLIN WATTS
LONDON•SYDNEY

First published in 2008 by Franklin Watts

Franklin Watts
338 Euston Road
London, NW1 3BH

Franklin Watts Australia
Level 17/207 Kent Street
Sydney, NSW 2000

Series editor: Sarah Peutrill
Art Director: Jonathan Hair
Design: Elaine Wilkinson
Researcher: Charlotte Wormald
Panels written by: Sarah Ridley
Photographs: Laurence Cendrowicz (unless otherwise stated)

The Author and Publisher would like to thank the interviewees for their
contributions to this book.

Picture credits: Amihays/Shutterstock: 13. John Birdsall/JohnBirdsall: 24,
25. Elena Grigorova/Shutterstock: 18. Hannah Marsh/JohnBirdsall: 27. Vova
Pomortzeff/Shutterstock: 12. Ken Schulze/Shutterstock: 16. Every attempt
has been made to clear copyright. Should there be any inadvertent
omission please apply to the publisher for rectification.

Dewey number: 616.85' 26

ISBN: 978 0 7496 7704 6

Printed in China

Franklin Watts is a division of Hachette Children's Books,
an Hachette Livre UK company.

# CONTENTS

# WHAT IS DEPRESSION?

Depression is a disturbed state of mind that you cannot rationalise or talk yourself out of. We understand that if something terrible and traumatic happens in life we will feel upset, miserable or even despairing. But it is a lot harder to understand depression that seems to go on and on. Or to understand it when it occurs for no obvious reason.

## Depression and young people

Ongoing depression can be very scary and upsetting for anyone, but particularly so for young people. Adults do not always understand that children may experience depression. Yet statistics show that 10% of children in Great Britain aged 5–16 have, at some time, suffered from a clinically recognisable mental disorder

and this frequently involves depression in some form. Twice as many boys as girls aged 5–10 have a mental disorder, while among 11–16-year-olds it is 13% of boys and 10% of girls.

In fact, if anything, young people may get depressed more than adults, according to YoungMinds, the young people's mental health charity. They point out that: "They are more dependent or vulnerable, less well defended and more sensitive to what is happening to them and around them." YoungMinds also say however that depression is not necessarily an entirely negative experience. "Feeling depressed is part of living, of dealing with the uncertainties of life. For children and young people it is part of finding out how to cope with the ups and downs of growing up."

Yet it is also vital to understand that if the feelings go on for months, to the point where they interfere a great deal with day-to-day living, then the condition should be taken seriously. Particularly as about 2% of children aged 12, and 4 or 5% of teenagers, suffer from a clinical condition and need specialist help.

## Depression triggers

Depression can be triggered by very common things, such as rejection by someone cared for; bullying; disliking the way one looks; parents arguing or not getting on; not being listened to; exam stress.

Research has shown that a young person who uses cannabis regularly or heavily is likely to suffer depression, and is at least twice as likely to develop psychosis, as one who does not.

Then there are the severely traumatic events some young people suffer, which may result in powerful psychological harm. These include sexual and physical abuse; emotional neglect so that they do not feel valued or which makes them feel excessively pressurised; the death of someone close; very angry or violent family breakdown; witnessing domestic violence. When these occur, young people are more likely to become seriously depressed.

In this state some children become desperate and attempt suicide. For some this is clearly a cry for help, but others genuinely want to kill themselves. Others self-harm and inflict pain on themselves to distract from the pain they feel inside.

## Identifying depression

While some children may become withdrawn, uncommunicative and sad with depression, others show signs of depression through erratic, difficult and anti-social behaviour and aggression. If you think you or someone you know may have depression it is important to try to seek appropriate help. There is a box below with things that may help you identify depression. There is also a list of organisations offering help in a wide range of ways, from helplines to counselling, on page 31.

## This book

This book features the stories of eight young people who describe their own experiences of depression. Interviewing them I was moved by their honesty and openness in talking about how they had come to recognise that they were depressed, and the ways they had lived with, and often come through, the experience. I learned a great deal about how young people today grapple with a complex world and how they find conviction about themselves when parents or others have damaged rather than built up their sense of themselves. I learned of great courage and listened to heart-warming wisdom, humour and insight.

I hope you will feel as I do that the young people here have done a very valuable thing in sharing their experiences so frankly. They have done so because they believe in speaking out, so that others who may be going through depression may benefit from their stories.

# SIGNS OF DEPRESSION

• Being extremely moody and irritable, and getting stuck this way. Losing interest in things you usually enjoy.

• Not being able to concentrate, not doing well at schoolwork even if you were doing fine before.

• Being very self-critical. Disliking your body and your personality.

• Becoming withdrawn and losing touch with friends.

• Feeling you are carrying the weight of the world and that you will never feel happy or good again.

• Not looking after yourself. Not eating enough or well. Or eating too much without enjoying it. Not bothering with hygiene.

• Sleeping badly or sleeping too much.

• Panic attacks and paranoia about how others are behaving towards you.

• Having suicidal thoughts. Attempting suicide.

# ALL ALONE

Indu, 21, went through a childhood of depression, unable to get help because her parents would not agree to it.

## Q Can you see why you might have become depressed as a child?

My dad was an alcoholic and abusive to my mum who was completely absorbed in taking care of him, and trying not to displease him. My elder sister, my brother and I didn't get much parental care. I can see now that my mother was very depressed herself. If I asked her for anything she would tell me I must cope by myself. I would get home from school and eat biscuits and drink water. It was rare for meals to be made. I remember feeling very sad all the time. I was always worried about what was going on with my parents.

"If I asked [my mum] for anything she would tell me I must cope by myself... I was always worried about what was going on with my parents."

> *"I asked myself if my depression was like a broken arm and if I did not get it 'fixed' would I be like an arm and never function properly again."*

##  Did you understand that you were depressed?

I was 12 when it was first acknowledged. I was aware of being angry and trying to make sense of life. Sometimes I felt these thoughts would literally become too much for me to carry and that I would break if I had to carry the weight any more. I started crying a lot and having panic attacks. I went to see the school nurse. She said I needed help and called my mother but she just said I was being silly and to get a grip. Without parental permission, the nurse could not get me help.

##  Where did that leave you?

When I was 14 I started imagining committing suicide. I could see nothing hopeful ahead. The picture my parents presented of the future was all-negative. I come from a culture where women just get married and I thought I'd end up with someone like Dad and have a really bad life.

##  How did it affect your health?

I became more and more exhausted. Getting up in the morning was a painful hassle. But I think I had fallen in love with my depression to the point where I didn't want a life without it. I feared letting it go and becoming someone else. But then something the school nurse said came to me: "Depression is like a broken arm; if you break it you go to a doctor to get it fixed, and then sooner or later it starts functioning again properly." I asked myself if my depression was like a broken arm and if I did not get it 'fixed' would I be like an arm and never function properly again. That was when I started to see myself as abnormal.

##  Did you cope with school and study?

I felt driven to succeed, as though my life depended on it. I got a bursary to a private school to do A' levels but I didn't do well. I broke down and my truly amazing teacher realised just how bad a state I was in and ▶

# PANIC ATTACKS

A panic attack is a sudden overwhelming feeling of fear. It can last for a few seconds or quite a lot longer. Although it can be very frightening, a panic attack is not dangerous. Symptoms can include feeling faint or dizzy, sweating or shivering, difficulty in breathing, chest pain, feeling sick, a feeling of unreality and terrible fear. It is not absolutely clear why some people experience panic attacks but general anxiety and stress, a major event or change of lifestyle can make them more likely.

urged me to get help. I was 18 by now so I took his advice and made the most crucial decision of my life in going for help. I was put on anti-depressants. The first kind weren't right for me but the second were and after a few weeks I felt better. My basic personality didn't change but I could feel pleasure, I could work well and people around started telling me I was really a joyful person. It was as though the real me, repressed for years, had space to breathe. I told people I was on anti-depressants because I think it's important there shouldn't be a stigma and I want others to get the help I did.

## Q So did feeling better help you realise your goals?

I got a place at university to do philosophy, which is tough, but I love it. I decided then I was ready to come off the anti-depressants. I joined the Philosophical Society and had the confidence to speak and make my mark. But I go to counselling. I feel there is a lot of healing still to be done and I would go back on the anti-depressants if I went badly down again. Some people see medication as a failure but for me it is a liberation of the real me.

## Q How do you see the future now?

I want to do existential psychotherapy after university and I think my life experience will help with this. I am also able to see my parents with more understanding and I have quite a good relationship with my mother. I understand that it is up to me to be my own saviour when life is tough and I know now I won't give up on myself. ∎

# LOVE'S LOST

Cato, 25, went into depression during university with the breakdown of his first real relationship.

**Q How did you feel when you started university?**

I was happy and excited and feeling good with myself. In the first term I met Lucy* and we developed a strong emotional connection. We shared a lot of interests. It became very important for both of us and went on like this for the first year-and-a-half of university.

**Q So when did things begin to go wrong?**

I loved Lucy but I also felt I was young and missing the opportunity to be free, as my peers were. I began to feel a lot of conflict.

**Q So where did these feelings lead?**

I fantasised about going out with other girls and felt restless. I remember deciding I must end our relationship. I planned what to say and cut off my feelings so I could get the message across. Lucy was very upset.

**Q But you thought it was the right thing?**

I imagined I'd feel relieved but actually I felt very miserable at breaking the strong bond we had. We saw each other around a lot and I really missed her. She was unhappy too so after a few weeks we decided to try again.

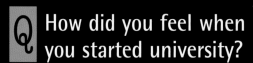

"I imagined I'd feel relieved but actually I felt very miserable at breaking the strong bond we had."

* Not her real name.

## So were things stronger with you and Lucy at this time?

At first it felt great. But really it was too early to get back together. All the pain of the break-up was still there and I had broken Lucy's trust.

 ## So what happened?

I realised that getting back hadn't been such a good idea, so I ended it again. Quite understandably Lucy was very angry with me. But even so she went on seeing me as a friend, which was surprisingly lovely. It took the pressure off us and Lucy was extremely generous in being sweet and affectionate towards me. We spent a lot of time building a good friendship and I felt very close to her.

 ## So did you imagine you could re-build the affair?

Not at first but slowly I saw that I really loved Lucy and we had something very special. In due course I wanted to try once more being a couple. But she said no and that felt like an enormous rejection. I can see how illogical that was but it was how I felt all the same. Then she started an affair with someone else. I felt betrayed which was obviously very selfish.

 ## So what happened with you then?

I felt completely powerless and desperate. The tables had turned. She was very much in control and I felt utterly diminished. I lost sight of how she could ever have loved me. I saw myself as worthless. Plus there was the terrible frustration of knowing I had destroyed the thing I really wanted. I thought about Lucy all the time and tried to think of ways I could make it OK again. I became obsessed, intent on fixing the unfixable and I felt I was going mad. I lost weight, developed stomach pains.

 ## Did you think you were depressed?

I didn't identify it as that. But I think my parents did and they were supportive. I was very tearful and the things that used to be pleasurable weren't any longer. I felt very scared.

## Did you get help?

I tried going to psychologists and I read a lot of self-help books offering solutions. Some of it helped a bit. My male friends thought I should get on with getting over Lucy and move on. But the irony was that, having had success with girls before, now they didn't want me. I think I gave off mega amounts of neediness.

"I lost sight of how she could ever have loved me. I saw myself as worthless. Plus there was the terrible frustration of knowing I had destroyed the thing I really wanted."

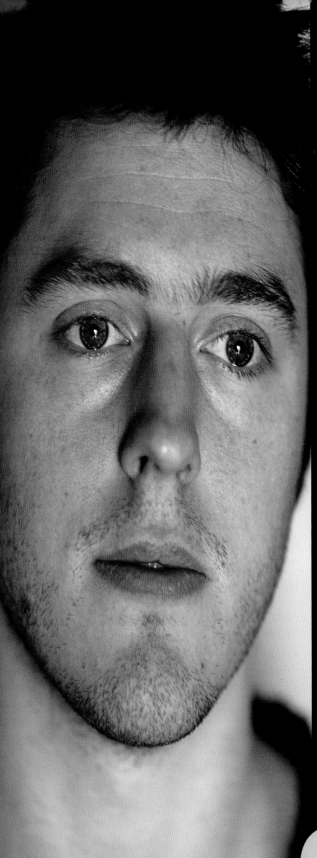

## SELF-HELP

Many people find they can help themselves out of depression. It is a good start to talk to someone about what is making them feel depressed or low. This can be a trusted friend, a member of the family, or a doctor, counsellor or a support group. There are many leaflets, books and websites about depression. It also helps to find ways to have fun and to relax – focus on hobbies, accept invitations to go out, listen to music, watch a favourite television programme or read a book. Eating a healthy diet and avoiding too much alcohol helps, as does taking exercise.

*"I was very tearful and the things that used to be pleasurable weren't any longer."*

## Q Did things improve?

When I left university and came back to London, I wasn't seeing Lucy around and a change of context really helped. But the wound didn't heal completely and I don't think it ever will because that first love is part of who I am and what I have become. But I'm over the extreme sadness and sense of futility. I went to Spain for several months and studied the language and then I took a post-graduate degree. Both helped me move on. I now have a new relationship. I am not depressed any more and I like to think I've learnt a lot emotionally. ■

# DRUG-TAKING DEPRESSION

Gary*,17, suffered depression as a result of his drug-taking. Dance helped him quit and he now works for a performing arts organisation.

*Not his real name, photo posed by model.

I got into difficulties when I moved to high school. I found the work hard and the teachers weren't the nicest. I walked out in the second year, when I was 13. My parents were near to killing me. We had a lot of fights about me not going to school. They were worried I'd just be a layabout and my dad was ambitious for me. He always regretted not getting a better education himself.

## Smoking cannabis

I started smoking a good deal of cannabis and it took me out of myself but also de-motivated me. Looking back I can see that I became very low and depressed. I spent a lot of time just hanging about.

*"I spent a lot of time just hanging about."*

During this time my parents got me a place at a guidance centre for kids out of school. I had an interview and the teachers were really nice so I spent a year there, but I was taking drugs all the time and then someone introduced me to ecstasy and I loved it. I usually took about five in an evening, but sometimes more. I paid for the drugs with money I earned spray painting cars and doing other chores.

## Drifting

But a lot of the time I felt very drained and depressed. I didn't put it down to the drugs then – or perhaps I preferred not to as they were the thing giving me pleasure in life. I knew I was drifting and my parents' disappointment in me made me feel really bad. I had no idea what I would do with my life.

Then I was introduced to a man running a performing arts group and he invited me to join. There was a lot of physical exercise and it was really hard for me because I was so unfit. But I liked what the group was doing and I really wanted to go on.

## Quitting drugs

The man running it guessed I was on drugs because my reactions were slow and I didn't look fit. Basically he told me I had talent and might be able to work on projects with them when I had trained – but I had to choose between that and drugs. They said they would help me quit and that is what they did by keeping me really busy, and being there to talk to whenever I felt tempted to go back to the drugs.

*"The depression and sense of hopelessness are just a memory."*

It's two years since I last had any drugs, although there were a few lapses getting there. The depression and sense of hopelessness are just a memory. I'm happy and excited by life these days. My parents are a lot happier too. ■

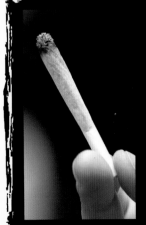

# CANNABIS AND DEPRESSION

Cannabis contains chemicals that can have effects on various areas of the brain. While it can make someone feel relaxed and happy, if that person is already feeling low or anxious, it can make these feelings worse. Most doctors and scientists believe there is a link between using cannabis regularly as a teenager and feeling depressed or anxious. They don't all agree as to whether the cannabis actually caused these feelings or whether it just made them worse. Cannabis can also make it hard for some teenagers to focus on schoolwork or other activities, giving them few opportunities to succeed and feel happy.

# ACCEPTING THE PAST

Lois, 20, was adopted and has been depressed as long as she can remember. She now does campaigning work for young people with depression.

## Q Were you a contented child?

I was adopted aged one, although I didn't know that until I was four. My adoptive parents were actually lovely to me, and I did feel close to my dad, a vicar. But I gave my mum a lot of grief. I didn't talk to her and I was physically nasty. I was convinced she hated me compared to her biological child. I know now she would have been loving and would have cuddled me if I'd let her, but I wouldn't. Apart from this, I kept everything inside me and even when I smiled and laughed and was happy on top the dark feeling was there. I think I've been depressed as long as I can remember.

*"I know now [my mum] would have been loving and would have cuddled me if I'd let her, but I wouldn't. I think I've been depressed as long as I can remember."*

> *"I wondered about my real mother all the time. What was she doing? Was she married? Was she Madonna?"*

## Q Although you couldn't remember your mother, did you think about her?

I wondered about my real mother all the time. What was she doing? Was she married? Was she Madonna? All I knew was that I had an elder sister who wasn't adopted. I thought there must be something very bad about me and that was why she didn't want me.

## Q Did you feel it would help to find your natural mother?

When I was 16 I felt I must know more. I learned my parents had split. My mother was unmarried when she got pregnant with me but I couldn't trace her. At that time I plunged into despair.

> *"I took my first overdose of pills … when I was eight."*

## Q How bad was your depression?

I took my first overdose of pills from the medicine cabinet when I was eight although they only made me feel unwell. After that there were a lot of other attempts later on. I had been hurting myself for years, ever since I can remember, but I only started cutting myself when I was 16. I kept the scars from everyone.

## Q Did anything change during your teens?

Until I finished GCSEs and left school I was popular and liked going out with friends. But over the summer holidays my depression got worse. I went into a bingeing and vomiting cycle and lost a huge amount of weight. I became very withdrawn and weak and I couldn't work when I got to sixth form. My parents put my weight loss down to teenage changes. And the teachers didn't seem to notice. But I told the RE teacher in confidence that I was struggling. He said he was there if I ever needed him, and that was a help. ▶

## BULIMIA

Bulimia is an eating disorder where someone craves food and 'binge-eats' – eating a lot of food quickly, and often secretly – yet is obsessed with being slim. This can lead to feeling guilt, disgust and a desire to get rid of the food by vomiting or by taking laxatives. The person may feel a sense of calm and control at this point, but soon feelings of disgust and low self-esteem return. It is not clear what causes bulimia but low self-esteem, a terrible event or poor relationships can contribute. Bulimia can lead to tooth decay, sore throats, stomach aches, tiredness and depression. Many people cure themselves but some people need to seek help from a doctor.

## Q Did you begin to feel better?

No. While I was working on A' levels I attempted to overdose again and I was admitted to The Priory adolescent ward, but was discharged after three months when I turned 17. I overdosed again and was put into an adult ward and sectioned for 18 months. I was diagnosed with depression and psychotic features. It was a locked ward, with a lot of very psychotic and frightening people. It was no place for a young person. I didn't get better at all.

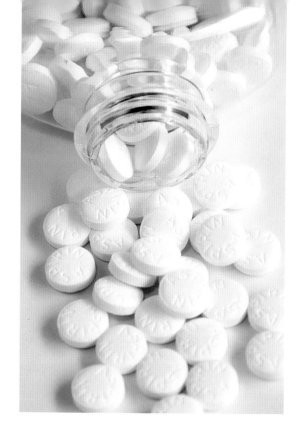

> "It was a locked ward, with a lot of very psychotic and frightening people."

## Q So what happened then?

I was referred to a place in York called The Retreat, a therapeutic community with very intense work on yourself and your relationships. It was tiring and difficult, but I learned a lot about dealing with distress and regulating emotions.

## Q How did your parents react?

They were horrified to learn what I had been going through and said they felt terrible failures. They went to huge lengths to prove they really loved me. They visited me every day and have been as supportive as they can be ever since.

# DEPRESSION AND ADOPTION

While many adopted children feel happy with their adoptive family, some find it hard to cope with being adopted. They feel a continuing sense of loss, grief, rejection, separation anxiety or even anger relating to their birth mother. As a result, it can be difficult to form a close relationship with the adoptive parents, which can lead to feeling isolated and depressed. Adoption support workers, school teachers or family members can try to help with some of these issues.

> "When I was 18 I went to a presentation on adoption and learned how common depression is in adopted people because that vital early attachment with the mother is severed abruptly."

## Q Did you come to understand why you felt so bad by this time?

When I was 18 I went to a presentation on adoption and learned how common depression is in adopted people because that vital early attachment with the mother is severed abruptly. Understanding this helped me in turn to understand why I had been so angry with my adoptive mum.

## Q Do you feel there is anything to be gained from your experience?

I have been able to make something valuable of the experience since becoming involved with a mental health charity, YoungMinds. I contributed to a report on young people being put into adult wards, called 'Pushed Into The Shadows', which they were doing. I was asked to be part of a board of young people they were setting up to contribute to campaigning work. It gives all those years of depression a meaning. It's not about me being tortured for nothing but so that I can be a help to other young people. ■

# YEARS OF DEPRESSION

Bella*, 22, had an unstable childhood and in her teens she had a breakdown. Therapy and joining a group of others with mental health problems helped her through.

*Not her real name, photo posed by model.

My parents separated when I was six weeks old and my mum and I moved in with my grandparents. My mum met my stepfather when I was five and moved out to live with him, leaving me. I felt very abandoned and within a few years I had become difficult and my grandparents didn't know what to do with me. I was sent to boarding school.

## Running away

I was difficult at age 14. I became quite aggressive and withdrawn and I kept running away from home. I didn't seem to be able to get on with anyone.

"I was difficult at age 14. I became quite aggressive and withdrawn and I kept running away from home."

When I left I felt hollow inside, as though there was nobody there for me and I became very rebellious. I moved into my boyfriend's house, but I felt depressed as hell inside and he found it very difficult. I was 16 at the time and in sixth form. Suddenly I couldn't function. I had a phobia about being with people.

## Afraid to go out

I was referred to the Community Practice Nurse at my doctor's. But I only got appointments weeks apart and I was getting worse, staying indoors, sometimes in bed, all the time. Then, when I was 18, I was put into an adult psychiatric service and that was horrible. I was among shockingly sick people and I just thought, 'I shouldn't be here'.

Eventually I saw a psychiatrist who told me I needed a hobby to get me out and functioning – and there I was unable to leave the house!

"I was able to look at why I was so angry and hostile to people who wanted to care for me."

## Understanding the problems

After a while the psychiatrist got me a place with a psychotherapist and that was the best move ever, although at first I hated going. But over time I connected with her, and I was able to look at why I was so angry and hostile to people who wanted to care for me. I felt the process gave me tools for dealing with the feelings although it was a slow process. Then I joined a group of other young people with mental health problems and it was so valuable seeing that I was not alone with my condition. Sharing our experiences helped me a lot.

"Sharing our experiences helped me a lot."

I have come a long way since then. I'm now doing a youth work course. I think once you have had mental health problems you are always susceptible and I have down days. But I also have perspective and know things will change for the better again. ■

## PSYCHIATRIC SERVICES

When depression does not go away after a few weeks, young people need to seek help from their family doctor or a nurse. They may be given an appointment with a specialist, such as a psychologist, a counsellor or a psychiatrist. These health professionals will draw up a plan for regular meetings (counselling or therapy). This will help to find out the cause of the depression and suggest ways to overcome it. Most people do not need to stay in hospital.

# MANAGING MELTDOWN

As a child and teenager, Nick had wildly fluctuating moods. In his mid–30s he was finally diagnosed with bipolar disorder (manic depression).

## Q Was there anything to suggest this disorder in your childhood?

I wet my bed regularly until my teens. I had, and still have, very vivid and often disturbing dreams. I remember being obsessed with the labels in clothes and most mornings I would try on up to ten pairs of pants, vests and shirts until I settled on a pair that felt comfortable. My school reports at junior school regularly said I was easily distracted.

"I had, and still have, very vivid and often disturbing dreams. I remember being obsessed with the labels in clothes..."

"I can remember hyperactive behaviour like throwing myself down escalators for the fun of it. But then I would withdraw and just want to hide away."

## Q Did you cope all right with school?

I took exams. I was extremely sociable with a lot of friends but I was also very full on. I can remember hyperactive behaviour like throwing myself down escalators for the fun of it. But then I would withdraw and just want to hide away.

## Q Do you have a good relationship with your parents and are you surprised they didn't see anything to worry about?

I had a very good childhood with loving parents. But less was known about mental health issues then and my behaviour probably seemed strange rather than worrying. ▶

# BIPOLAR DISORDER

This condition affects people's moods, which can swing from feeling extremely low and depressed for a few weeks, to feeling on a high and full of energy (manic) for the next few weeks. Some people with bipolar disorder will only experience extreme mood swings a couple of times in their lifetime, remaining stable the rest of the time, whilst others experience many highs and lows. Medicines can help to control the condition and sufferers can learn to recognise what might trigger it off.

## Q Were your mood changes very obvious by this time?

I think a lot of it was put down to my being a teenager but bipolar illness frequently shows up in the late teens and early 20s. My university friends tell me I had profound personality swings. When I was high I would stay up all night walking around campus. My head would be full of hectic thoughts and I went to lectures in the day. Then came the dreadful downs. After a manic period I'd feel utterly exhausted as though nothing were left inside me, my speech would be slurred and I felt very groggy. All I wanted to do was sleep and sometimes I would disappear to bed for three days at a time.

## Q Did your behaviour contribute to your mental health problems?

I got into a band when I was at university and I was doing drugs – cannabis and quite a lot of acid. It seems crazy now and I feel sure the drugs altered my brain chemistry and made my illness worse. I went on working in music after university and working with studios and doing jobs such as in a call centre, which I hated, to earn a living. It was very stressful. After a year I snapped. I quit the job, left the band, split up with a long-term girlfriend – all in the course of two weeks. I went into a dark, hopeless state and completely shut off from everyone. I hardly left home for a month. I lost a lot of weight, lost hair and I had no sense of reality.

## Q Did you realise you needed help?

I went to the doctor's, to casualty departments and to psychiatric nurses. I was crying out for help. I was put on anti-depressants and then I had anxiety attacks. I ended up being put in a psychiatric ward and although a lot about it was grim I did realise there were others who were going through what I was. I learned the importance of sharing experiences

# DEPRESSION AND FAMILIES

The exact cause of much mental illness remains unknown. However, some mental illnesses, like physical illnesses, are more common in some families than others. Alongside this, children who live in a family where someone suffers mental illness are likely to have a more difficult childhood, which in turn could lead to them suffering mental ill-health as they grow up. Despite this, it is far more likely that someone will not develop mental illness, despite their family history, than that they will.

> "I read lots of books and articles on mental health because I believe that knowledge is the way forward."

with others, and I have gone on doing that. I read lots of books and articles on mental health because I believe that knowledge is the way forward. I am a volunteer for Equilibrium – the Bipolar Foundation – because I want to use my experience to help others.

## Q Bipolar disorder is known to have a genetic link. Does anyone else in your family suffer from it?

A few years ago I learnt that my mother had suffered post-natal depression. Then a couple of years ago a cousin was going through a bad time and she told me that, when she was in her 20s, she had a breakdown and was put into hospital. I think it would have helped me to understand, sooner, that I needed to go to a doctor, if I had known this.

## Q How did your bipolar diagnosis come about?

I had been diagnosed as ordinarily depressed but when my girlfriend Tanya first met me I was very withdrawn, then the second time I was absolutely in her face. She wrote to a psychiatrist describing my behaviour and I was finally properly diagnosed. I now have proper medication and a wonderful psychiatrist who really helps me.

## Q So are things better?

It makes a big difference knowing that what I have is a recognised condition. I still have extreme mood swings but I am better at managing them. And Tanya and I have a baby daughter. That has convinced me that life is worth living. ■

23

# PUSHY PARENT

Nettie*, 16, was pressurised by her mother and her suppressed anger turned into depression.

*Not her real name, photo posed by model.

My parents are from Asia but I was born and brought up in Britain. I am the eldest of three children and for as long as I can remember there has been pressure from my mother to perform very well academically. I have always had to study when other children had free time so it hasn't been easy to have friends. And it seemed nothing I did was ever good enough.

## Controlling

When I did my GCSEs and got ten As, six of them starred, my mother was angry that I hadn't got all A stars. She beat me when I was little if I didn't do as she said, and there were times when she forced me to eat. She wanted to control everything in my life.

"... for as long as I can remember there has been pressure from my mother to perform very well academically."

"I began to feel very black and hopeless.
I started wanting to cut myself but I didn't do it.
I knew, somehow, it might make me feel even worse."

One of the hardest things was when a girl I was very close to fell out of favour with my mother. I'm not sure why but I was not allowed to have anything more to do with her. I became very depressed. My father wouldn't challenge my mother but I sensed he empathised with me and that helped a bit.

My mother was determined I must be a doctor and went on about it all the time, but it wasn't what I wanted. I began to feel very black and hopeless. I started wanting to cut myself but I didn't do it. I knew, somehow, it might make me feel even worse. It didn't occur to me to find someone to talk to but a teacher, who knew a bit about how upset I have been, asked me if I'd like to see the school counsellor.

## Talking it through

I felt I could talk to the counsellor and that she would understand and not judge. It was such a relief to get the feelings of anger and desperation out from inside me. And as I talked about feeling my mother never wanted to understand me, but just to have me show the world how clever her daughter was, the counsellor helped me see that I was allowed to be angry about this.

I only had a few sessions with the counsellor, but because she heard how I was brimming with emotions and fury that seemed to stop me moving on, I started looking into possibilities for the future that could please my mother and also myself. I went to an open day for a university course on paediatrics and realised how much I wanted to work with children.

That was a turning point. I was able to tell my parents I would do medicine, but also I had made a choice for myself and that was so important. But I don't think this would have happened if I hadn't had the chance to express my anger and upset to the counsellor. If I have difficulties at university I will certainly go for further help. ∎

# ATTEMPTED SUICIDE

Louisa*, 13, has a brother with Asperger's syndrome who made her so unhappy she attempted suicide.
*Not her real name

## Q Do you have siblings you are close to?

I have an elder sister and a 16-year-old brother who has Asperger's. He and I have a difficult relationship. As I grew up he picked on me and argued with me a lot. And there were times when he was physically threatening.

## Q Did your parents know about this?

They knew I got upset but I didn't want to worry them with how bad things were because I knew they were having a really hard time with my brother who is very active and physical. So I shut myself away a lot and I don't think they realised I felt so miserable inside.

## Q Was school a place you felt better?

I had some good friends, but I had no confidence about myself, so I couldn't really see why friends would like me. And I was always struggling with schoolwork. I found it very hard to concentrate.

## Q Was that a problem?

It was because all my friends got into grammar school and I didn't and I felt very, very bad about that. I felt more useless than ever but I couldn't tell my parents because they were really stressed trying to get my brother into a residential school.

## Q How did you deal with these feelings?

I began cutting myself a bit on my arms but I kept it well hidden and my mum didn't know. ▶

# SELF-HARM

Self-harm describes the ways that some people harm themselves to achieve relief from overwhelming emotions. The most common form of self-harm is to make cuts to the upper arm or thigh, where no one will be able to see them. Other ways are to inflict burns or bruises, pull out hair or take some pills. It is not usually the intention to commit suicide. Many self-harmers do not really know why they do it but feel a release and a sense of control over their difficult lives or desperate feelings when they do so. It is important to seek help from a trained counsellor or health professional.

*"I began cutting myself a bit on my arms but I kept it well hidden and my mum didn't know."*

Photo posed by model.

And I stopped eating. My mum realised I was losing weight and she talked to me about how dangerous it was. Mum was worried enough to take me to the doctor, who referred me to the local Child and Adolescent Mental Health Service (CAMHS). I saw a psychiatrist and he recognised that I was depressed and talked about counselling. But I felt trapped in my life and couldn't see how it would get better. I took an overdose of painkillers and ended up in hospital. The nurse said I was attention-seeking. I was assigned a social worker and sent home. I felt really selfish that I'd hurt my mum and dad so much and was worried they would think they had failed as parents.

## Q What happened that made things worse?

I went on holiday with my family and my brother just wound me up all the time and he went on and on saying horrible things. One day I had a huge row with him. My parents knew how hard it was for me, but there wasn't much they could do and I just felt at breaking point. I went to my room to cool-off but I felt I couldn't take any more. I went into the bathroom and found a lot of paracetamol and other pills sold over the counter and I made myself swallow them all.

> "I found a lot of
> paracetamol and … I made
> myself swallow them all."

# RESIDENTIAL PSYCHIATRIC CARE

Sometimes, when a young person's depression or other mental illness becomes serious, counselling and therapy on a weekly basis are not enough to improve their condition, or keep them safe. The young person may be encouraged to enter a residential psychiatric unit. There will be several young people with different or similar conditions in the unit. By becoming involved in therapy through group work, with their family or on their own, the young person can receive professional help with their problem. There will also be opportunities to study and learn new skills. Where possible, the psychiatric unit will be as close to home as possible so that the family and the school can remain involved. Most people only stay for a few weeks, rather than months.

## Q Clearly you didn't succeed in killing yourself, so what happened?

My sister came in and found me in a darkened bedroom. She went on at me until I told her what I had done and she called an ambulance. I ended up in hospital for the second time, aged 12. I remember my mother being so shocked and saying she realised how hard it was for me with my brother, and that she felt I was in a very lonely place.

## Q As this was your second overdose, did the doctors take it seriously?

I was admitted to Collingham Gardens, a residential psychiatric unit for children and young people. They take the youngest and most disturbed children. I didn't want to go but my parents saw it as a chance for me to be helped, and I didn't want to hurt them any more, so I went. I hated it at first and tried to run away, because they challenged some of my behaviour and the whole place works on getting you to open up and look at yourself.

But then I settled and made some good friends. I started liking the way the staff help you understand why you feel so depressed and they are very positive and give praise when you do well. My parents were involved in my treatment. They visited twice a week and I went home for weekends. I got much closer to them and now it's much easier to talk to them about how I feel.

## Q How long did you stay there?

I was there for four months and I was nervous about leaving. I was frightened that I would slip back into my depression, which had got much better at Collingham. But my brother is in a boarding school and when he's at home he's easier to be with than he was. I am back in school and coping with that. I would like to say everything is absolutely better, but it's not. I still get bad down moods but I have been taught skills for dealing with them and I can feel some optimism about the future. ■

# GLOSSARY

**acid**
The street name for lysergic acid diethylamide, a powerful illegal drug that causes hallucinations and a feeling of euphoria.

**anti-depressants**
Drugs that are prescribed to ease the symptoms of depression and anxiety disorders.

**Asperger's syndrome**
A genetic disorder thought to be similar to autism. People with Asperger's syndrome have difficulties in three main areas: socialising, communication and behaviour.

**bipolar disorder**
A disorder that causes a person to experience periods of mania and depression. See page 21.

**bursary**
Funds given to help students who meet specific eligibility criteria and have financial need.

**cannabis**
An illegal drug – considered a soft drug, it consists of the dried leaves of the hemp plant; smoked or chewed for euphoric effect.

**counselling**
A therapy in which a trained person listens to people's problems and anxieties, and advises without judging, to help them find their own answers.

**ecstasy**
Ecstasy is the name given to the illegal drug MDMA.

**existential psychotherapy**
A theory of individual psychology concentrating on freedom and responsibility. It is a system highlighting the role of responsibility and free choice in the direction of a person's life.

**genetic**
Describing features or conditions of the body that are the result of hereditary – traits passed down from parent to child through genes.

**hyperactive**
Unusually overactive. Extreme difficulty sitting still, fidgetiness, excessive running.

**laxatives**
Medications that are prescribed to relieve long-term constipation, but which are sometimes abused in order to lose weight.

**paediatrics**
The branch of medicine that deals with diagnosis, treatment and prevention of diseases in children.

**paracetamol**
A drug that is used for the relief of fever, headaches, and other minor aches and pains.

**post-natal depression**
A mental illness that can occur within the weeks or months after childbirth.

**psychiatric nurse**
A special nurse who cares for people of all ages with mental illness or mental distress.

**psychiatrist**
A medical doctor who specialises in the diagnosis and treatment of mental disorders.

**psychologist**
A non-medical specialist in the diagnosis and treatment of mental and emotional problems. Their role involves testing, counselling and/ or psychotherapy, without the use of drugs.

**psychotherapist**
A therapist who uses a set of techniques to try to cure or improve psychological and mental health problems. The commonest form of psychotherapy is direct contact between the therapist and patient, mainly talking.

**psychotic**
When a person is suffering from severe mental illness and loses contact with reality.

**sectioned**
A person is sectioned when they are detained, under the Mental Health Act, for hospital treatment.

**self-harm**
Deliberate injury to one's own body. This injury may be aimed at distracting the person from unbearable emotions or for other reasons.

# FURTHER INFORMATION

## CALM (Campaign Against Living Miserably)
Free helpline: 0800 58 58 58
Web: www.thecalmzone.net
*Advice for young men aged 16-35 suffering from depression.*

## Capio Helpline
Free helpline: 0800 733 094
Web: www.florencenightingale hospitals.co.uk
*Advice on anorexia or bulimia, addictions, depression etc.*

## Careline
Tel: 0845 122 8622
Web: www.carelineuk.org
*Telephone counselling for people of any age, on any issue.*

## ChildLine
Free helpline: 0800 1111
Web: www.childline.org.uk
*Telephone counselling for any child with any problem.*

## Depression Alliance
Tel: 020 7633 0557
Web: www.depressionalliance.org
*Help to people with depression, run by sufferers themselves. Helps members to form self-help groups.*

## Fellowship of Depressives Anonymous
Tel: 01702 433838
*Support for sufferers on a self-help/mutual-support basis.*

## Get Connected
Free helpline: 0808 808 4994
Web: www.getconnected.org.uk
*Helpline for young people.*

## MDF The Bipolar Organisation
Tel: 020 7793 2600
Web: www.mdf.org.uk
*For people with bipolar disorder.*

## Parents Association for the Prevention of Young Suicide
Web: www.papyrus-uk.org
*An organisation committed to the prevention of young suicide.*

## National Self-Harm Network
Web: www.nshn.co.uk
*Support for people who self-harm.*

## Rethink
Helpline: 020 8974 6814
Web: www.rethink.org
*Services to carers and people with severe mental illness.*

## Samaritans
Tel: 08457 90 90 90
Web: www.samaritans.org.uk
*Support for anyone in crisis.*

## SANE
Tel: 08457 678000
Web: www.sane.org.uk
*For sufferers, friends and relatives affected by mental illness.*

## There4me
Web: www.there4me.com
*Email support service for young people between 12-16 years.*

## Threshold Women's Mental Health Infoline
Web: www.thresholdwomen.org.uk
*Information for those concerned about women's mental health (16+).*

## Youth Access
Helpline: 020 8896 3675
Web: www.youthaccess.org.uk
*Counselling services for young people aged 12–25 years.*

## Youth2Youth
Helpline telephone: 020 8896 3675
Web: www.youth2youth.co.uk
*Email and telephone support, run by young volunteers for under 19s.*

www.acp.uk.net
*Holds a directory of child psychotherapists – fee paying.*

www.counselling.co.uk
*Provides details of local counsellors and psychotherapists – fee paying.*

www.bps.org.uk
*Holds a register of chartered psychologists – fee paying.*

www.psychotherapy.org.uk
*Provides details of local counsellors and psychotherapists – fee paying.*

www.bipolar-foundation.org
*Works to improve the treatment and understanding of bipolar disorder.*

www.youngminds.org.uk
*The young people's mental health charity.*

www.thesite.org
*Articles on young people's issues including health and wellbeing.*

www.kidshelp.com.au
Free helpline: 1800 55 1800
*Telephone and online counselling for young people under 25.*

www.youthline.co.nz
Free helpline: 0800 37 66 33
*Support for young people in New Zealand.*

# INDEX

## TALKING POINTS

The interviews in this book may provoke a range of reactions: shock, sympathy, empathy, sadness. As many of the interviewees found, talking can help you to sort out your emotions. If you wish to talk about the interviews here are some questions to get you started:

### Indu's story - page 6

Why do you think Indu fell 'in love with' depression? Indu says she was told that depression is like a broken arm – it can be fixed. Do you agree? Indu finds medication helpful but says some people see it as a failure. Why do people have this attitude towards anti-depressants?

### Cato's story - page 9

Cato's male friends thought he should 'get on with getting over' his girlfriend. Do you think boys and girls react to depression in other people in different ways? Why is it generally harder for men to talk about their feelings?

### Gary's story - page 12

Cannabis in some countries is seen as a 'softer' drug than others. Does this encourage young people to think it doesn't have dangers and side effects? If it's proved cannabis does cause depression in young people, should it be re-classified?

### Lois's story - page 14

Why do you think depression is common in adopted children? Lois was told she was adopted at the age of four. When do you think is the right time to explain?

### Bella's story - page 18

How do you think sharing experiences helps people with depression? Does it help you to talk about your problems?

### Nick's story - page 20

Nick's depression was finally diagnosed as bipolar disorder and knowing he has this recognised condition seems to help him. Why do you think this is?

### Nettie's story - page 24

How much do you think Nettie's depression was her mother's fault? What do you think her mother's side of the story might have been?

### Louisa's story - page 26

Why was it so hard for Louisa when she first went for treatment? Self-harm is a very extreme form of depression but seems to be increasing in Britain. Why do you think this might be?

# HOW TO SURVIVE IN THE
# RAINFOREST

ANGELA ROYSTON

WAYLAND
www.waylandbooks.co.uk

First published in Great Britain in 2018 by Wayland
Copyright © Hodder & Stoughton, 2018.
All rights reserved.

Produced for Wayland by Calcium Creative Ltd
Editors: Sarah Eason and Jennifer Sanderson
UK Editor: Sarah Ridley
Designer: Simon Borrough
Cover design: Cathryn Gilbert

ISBN: 978 1 5263 0960 0

10 9 8 7 6 5 4 3 2 1

Wayland, an imprint of
Hachette Children's Group
Part of Hodder and Stoughton
Carmelite House
50 Victoria Embankment
London EC4Y 0DZ

An Hachette UK Company
www.hachette.co.uk
www.hachettechildrens.co.uk

Printed and bound in China

Photo Credits: Cover: Shutterstock: Wilm Ihlenfeld, Ana Vasileva. Inside: Dreamstime: Luis Louro
21t, Marco Regalia 8cl; Shutterstock: Ammit 16c, Bersanelli 27c, Ryan M. Bolton 18c, Calek 15t,
Hector Conesa 7tl, Bob Denelzen 9t, Empire331 23c, Frontpage 5c, 25cl, 29c, Markus Gann 10l,
22l, Robert Adrian Hillman 22c, Wilm Ihlenfeld 16l, 26l, Jakov 24cr, Peter Jochems 14c, Michael
Klenetsky 17c, Lightpoet 6cr, Reistlin Magere 4l, 18l, 28l, Christopher Meder Photography 12l, 24l,
PhotoHappiness 4br, RM 26c, Rsfatt 28c, Leonid Shcheglov 10c, Nickolay Stanev 12c, StillFX 24c,
Szefei 4c, 6l, 14l, Matt Tilghman 8l, Worldswildlifewonders 13cl; Jan Smith 11c.

# CONTENTS

# SURVIVAL!

**R**ainforests are beautiful but they are hot, sweaty and dangerous, too. You will need knowledge and skills to survive in a rainforest. You will also need to be able to put up with a lot of hardship!

Amazon rainforest

**AMAZON RAINFOREST**
**SIZE:** about 7 million square kilometres
**FACT:** it is the biggest rainforest in the world

The biggest, thickest rainforests grow in the **tropics**. It rains hard almost every day, so rainforests are hot and wet nearly all year round. These conditions are perfect for plants to grow, and for many kinds of animal to live. They are not so good for humans so only a few people live there.

Kamayura tribespeople

## KAMAYURA TRIBESPEOPLE
**HOW MANY TRIBES:** the Kamayura is one of 200 tribes in the Amazon rainforest
**SURVIVAL:** they make everything they need, even musical instruments

5

# HOW TO SURVIVE

A rainforest can provide everything you need to survive, including water, food, shelter and a raft. For food, there are fish in the rivers and birds and **tapirs** in the forest. You can build a shelter and a bed from bamboo and large leaves.

tapir

**TAPIR**
**WHERE:** Amazon and southeast Asian rainforests
**SIZE:** grows up to 1.2 m tall

Rainforests are also very dangerous places. Poisonous plants, dangerous insects and snakes are everywhere. Jaguars hide among the trees and caimans lurk in the water and. Caiman are similar to alligators. Keep a look out for these dangerous **predators**.

# TOUGH TIP

The best fruit is often high in the trees, but not always. Fruit falls from the trees to the ground, sometimes knocked down by chimpanzees and other animals. Be careful when picking up fallen fruit because it is likely to be crawling with insects.

chimpanzee

## CHIMPANZEE
**WHERE:** Congo rainforest in Africa
**HOW:** swings through the trees looking for food and comes down to the ground, where it uses sticks and other tools to catch **termites**

# DRINKING WATER

**T**here is no shortage of water in a rainforest, but it is not all safe to drink! The ground is often swampy and there are lots of streams. You can safely drink the water from mountain streams but not from rivers, pools and swamps.

rainforest stream

## AMAZON STREAMS AND TRIBUTARIES
**NUMBER OF STREAMS:** countless streams join together to form more than 1,000 **tributaries**
**LENGTH:** 17 of the tributaries are each more than 1,600 km long

## TOUGH TIP

Some vines contain a clean, safe supply of water in their stems, but not all of them. To check whether a vine is a water vine, cut off a section of the stem. If clear water runs out, and a drop of it tastes good, it is safe to drink.

You can also collect and drink rainwater. However, if the water has dripped off forest leaves, it can contain germs and make you ill. Boil it or **sterilise** it using water purifying tablets to make it safe to drink.

### RAINFALL IN THE RAINFOREST

**AMOUNT:** around 6,350 mm of rain a year
**WETTEST RAINFOREST:** Mount Waialeale, in Hawaii, gets about 11,430 mm of rain a year!

# SAFE TO EAT?

More different types of plant grow in the rainforest than anywhere else. This does not mean that there is plenty of food though, because many plants are poisonous. You have to know what you are eating!

Brazil nuts

**BRAZIL TREE**
**SIZE:** grows up to 50 m high
**USE:** Brazil nuts contain all the different types of nutrient a person needs

The best foods are fruit and nuts. Most of them grow high in the trees, out of reach, so you will need to climb to reach them. The trees grow so tall and thick that they block out the light for the plants below. Banana trees, however, have huge leaves that catch enough light to grow.

black bean plant

**BLACK BEAN PLANT**
**WHERE:** grows in rainforests in eastern Australia
**USE:** raw beans are poisonous, but are safe to eat when they have been ground into flour or roasted

# FOOD FROM ANIMALS

**F**inding meat in the rainforest is not easy. It is all about knowing what to look for. Wild turkeys and hens can be hunted on the forest floor. Rainforest people also eat monkeys and snakes.

Australian brush turkey

## BRUSH TURKEY
**SIZE:** grows up to 60 cm long
**USE:** a female brush turkey lays up to 24 eggs in a large mound. You can eat the eggs.

You can find food in rivers and lakes. Freshwater shrimps and small fish can be caught with nets. Tribespeople spear larger fish with sharp sticks. In Australia, **Aborigines** who live in the Australian rainforests make traps to catch eels.

spider monkey

**SPIDER MONKEY**
**WHERE:** Central and South America
**USE:** hunted for food by tribespeople using poison darts and blowpipes

13

# WATER FOR LIFE

**W**ith its never-ending rainfall, the rainforest has an abundance of rivers and streams. These are necessary for the survival of the rainforest tribespeople, providing them with food in the form of fish as well as fresh drinking water.

piranha fish

## PIRANHA FISH
**SIZE:** grows up to 46 cm long
**THREAT:** razor-sharp teeth rip prey to shreds in seconds

caiman

However, dangers lurk everywhere in the jungle, especially in the rivers. Here all sorts of wild creatures live, from giant snakes, such as the anaconda, to ferocious black caimans and small-but-deadly, flesh-stripping fish called piranhas.

# TOUGH TIP

No human can survive without water for more than three days, so stay close to freshwater sources, such as streams. Take care by the river's edge. Black caimans lie in wait for a victim to walk past the river. Caimans hunt and eat humans, picking off village children playing in the water or women washing clothes by the river's edge.

**CAIMAN**
**SIZE:** grows up to 6 m long
**THREAT:** lies hidden below the water, then attacks suddenly

15

# DANGER IN THE TREES

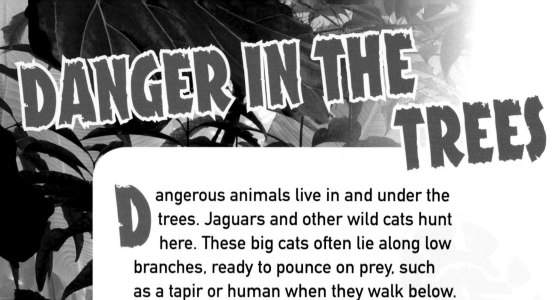

**D**angerous animals live in and under the trees. Jaguars and other wild cats hunt here. These big cats often lie along low branches, ready to pounce on prey, such as a tapir or human when they walk below. Snakes hang from vines, waiting for frogs and other prey to come within reach.

jaguar

## JAGUAR
**LENGTH:** grows up to 2—2.7 m long
**THREAT:** very strong jaws, which can bite through the shell of a turtle

16

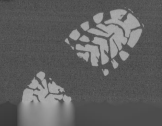

Some plants and animals protect themselves with poison. Poison dart frogs are easy to spot because of their bright colours. Whatever you do, do not touch them. Their skin is so poisonous, just one touch is enough to kill you.

poison dart frog

## POISON DART FROG

**SIZE:** grows up to 1.2 cm—6.3 cm long
**THREAT:** three different types of Amazonian poison dart frog are deadly to humans

# HEALTH HAZARDS

**K**eeping healthy is difficult in the rainforest. You can become very tired and can easily become ill. People are scared of poisonous spiders and snakes, such as the fer-de-lance, but the biggest threat is probably insects.

fer-de-lance

**FER-DE-LANCE**
**SIZE:** grows up to 2.4 m long
**THREAT:** extremely poisonous;
one bite can kill a human

Mosquitoes are insects that carry a serious disease called malaria. Other insects can burrow into your flesh and lay eggs, which hatch into **maggots**. Scratches and ordinary insect bites can quickly become **infected**.

## I SURVIVED

Chuck Klusman was the first US airman to be shot down during the Vietnam War. He was captured but managed to escape with Boun Mi, another prisoner. They walked over steep, jungle-covered mountains. Their worst problem was **leeches**. The leeches sucked their blood and made them weak. Luckily, the men managed to reach a friendly **outpost** and freedom.

mosquito

## MOSQUITO
**SIZE:** grows up to 1.9 cm long
**THREAT:** most likely to bite at night so always sleep under a mosquito net

19

# JUNGLE WEAR

The rainforest is hot, wet and full of spiky plants and poisonous creatures. You need to choose your clothes carefully. Make sure you cover your arms and legs with long sleeves and trousers. Many jungle survival experts even wear gloves.

jungle wear

**JUNGLE WEAR**
**PROTECTS AGAINST:** rain, scratches, insects, leeches, snakes and spiders
**RUCKSACK:** everything should fit into one bag

20

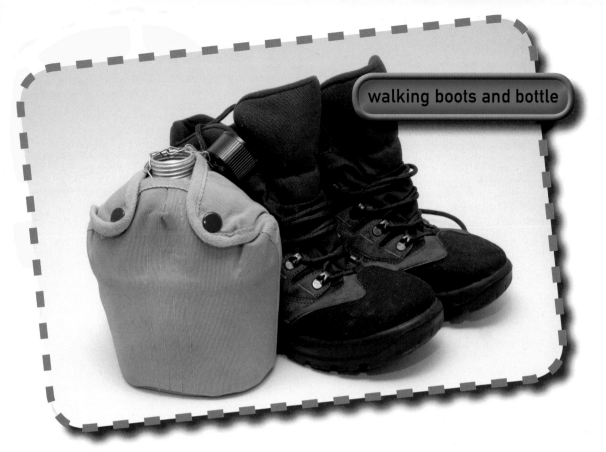

Strong boots are essential for wading through shallow water, and to protect against snake and spider bites. A rain cape is useful for when it rains. A hat is good protection from the rain and the sun. A hat will also keep insects that drop from the trees out of your hair.

**WALKING BOOTS AND FLASK**
**BOOTS:** need to be waterproof
**BOTTLE:** useful for storing clean water to drink

# TOUGH TIP

Shake out your boots before you put them on. Otherwise you might find a poisonous spider hiding in there! If you are bitten by a snake or spider, make sure you notice what it looks like so that the correct antidote can then be given to you.

**21**

# RAINFOREST KIT

**E**verything you take with you into the rainforest has to be carried in the same rucksack as your clothes. It is best to keep your kit to a minimum, but some items are vital. The first is a **machete**. This is needed to cut everything, from a path through the undergrowth to food to eat.

campsite

## CAMPSITE
**WHERE:** a clearing in the forest
**FIRE:** for boiling water, cooking and scaring off dangerous animals

The quickest way to make a bed is to hang a hammock between two trees, sheltered by a waterproof sheet (or rain cape) tied above it. The hammock should hang a metre above the ground, well away from snakes and insects on the ground below.

# TOUGH TIP

Do not forget these items:
- Machete
- Torch
- Matches or a lighter
- Map and compass
- Medicines
- Mosquito net
- Knife and spoon
- Cooking pot
- Water bottle

lighting a fire

## LIGHTING A FIRE
**WHAT YOU NEED:** dry leaves and wood to get the fire started
**HOW:** use matches or a lighter; strike a knife against a stone to create a spark or use a magnifying glass to focus the Sun's rays

23

# MAKING PROGRESS

There are no paths through the thickest rainforests. You will have to cut your own path using a machete. This takes a long time and is exhausting work. A much quicker way to travel is by boat. Some people even carry an **inflatable** boat with them.

machete

**MACHETE**
**SIZE:** blade is usually 30—60 cm long
**USE:** cutting through undergrowth, cutting wood, splitting coconuts, cutting cane, chopping up food

dugout canoe

# TOUGH TIP

Making a raft is easy in the rainforest. Use your machete to chop down several thick stems of bamboo. Cut them to the same length, and then tie them together with string, pulled from vines. Make paddles from flat wood and poles. The raft is ready to launch!

Local tribespeople use boats for fishing and to travel. They carve out a canoe from a thick branch or tree trunk, or they make a raft. Today, some villagers add an **outboard motor** to their canoe.

## DUGOUT CANOE
**SIZE:** around 2.4 m long, but can be up to 7.3 m long
**USES:** local people use smaller canoes for fishing, and for carrying goods and people

# WHICH WAY?

**F**inding your way in the rainforest is never easy. Thick undergrowth and tall trees make it impossible to see more than a short distance ahead. Rivers and streams may follow a winding course, making it hard to keep going in one direction.

Amazon river

**AMAZON RIVER**
**WHERE:** flows through the Amazon rainforest
**LENGTH:** 6,437 km

Explorers use a **Global Positioning Systems device** (GPS), which can tell them where they are, but not always which way to go! A map and compass help but sometimes there are no detailed maps. When all else fails, the best thing to do is to follow the flowing water of a stream or river until it reaches a settlement.

## I SURVIVED

Juliane Koepcke, a 17-year-old German girl, survived on her own in the Amazon rainforest for ten days after a plane crash in 1971. Luckily, Juliane's parents had taught her some survival skills. The streams provided Juliane with drinking water, so she managed to stay alive, despite not eating. She followed the streams downhill until, weak with hunger, she finally reached a hut by the river. Here she was found by some local men who led her to safety.

mountain gorilla

## MOUNTAIN GORILLA
**WHERE:** found in the Democratic Republic of Congo, in Africa
**SURVIVES:** feeds on leaves, shoots and fruit. Lives as part of a group usually made up of about 10 gorillas.

# GETTING HELP

The safest way to travel into the rainforest is to have a local guide. Local guides know the way through the forest as well as what is safe to eat and drink. They can also talk to other tribespeople you meet to tell them that you are not going to harm them.

Amazon tribesperson

## AMAZON TRIBESPEOPLE
**HOW MANY:** fewer than 250,000
**GROUPS:** about 200 tribal groups

## TOUGH TIP

Do not assume that rainforest tribespeople will be pleased to see you. Outsiders have destroyed large areas of rainforest, cutting down the trees on which the tribes rely. Do everything you can to show them that you are friendly.

When walkers are late in arriving at their destination, helicopters and rescuers may begin to search for them. If you are lost or need help, keep to the river. Look out for anyone who can help you. Light a fire to attract the attention of rescuers.

destroyed rainforest

## DESTROYED RAINFOREST

**HOW MUCH:** an area the size of England and Wales is destroyed each year
**WHY:** to grow crops, such as rubber trees and oil palms, and to graze cattle for beef

# GLOSSARY

**Aborigine** One of the native peoples of Australia. Aborigines lived in Australia long before people from Europe settled there.

**antidote** A medicine that treats poisons.

**cycad** A tropical plant that looks like a palm but produces its seeds in cones.

**Global Positioning Systems device** A device that helps find your location on a map.

**infected** Containing germs (bacteria) or other things that can cause illnesses.

**inflatable** Designed to be filled with air or gas before it is used.

**leech** A worm-like animal that sucks the blood of animals, including people.

**liana** A long, thick rainforest vine.

**machete** A large knife that is used to cut trees, bushes and crops.

**maggot** A small worm-like larva of a fly.

**outboard motor** A motor that is attached to the outside of a boat.

**outpost** A building or small settlement far away from any towns.

**predator** An animal that hunts and eats other animals.

**prey** An animal that is hunted and eaten by other animals.

**sterilise** To make something free from germs.

**tapir** A mammal that looks a bit like a pig with a trunk nose.

**termite** A small insect that eats wood.

**tributary** A small stream or river that flows into a larger river.

**tropics** The area between the Tropic of Cancer and the Tropic of Capricorn, which are imaginary lines drawn either side of the equator. The tropics are some of the hottest places on Earth.

# FURTHER READING

Simon Chapman, *Borneo Rainforest (Expedition Diaries),*
Franklin Watts 2018

Susie Brooks, *Where on Earth? Book of Rainforests,*
Wayland, 2015

Paul Calver and Toby Reynolds, *Rainforests (Visual Explorers),*
Franklin Watts, 2015

Paul Rockett. *30 Million Different Insects in the Rainforest (The Big Countdown),*
Franklin Watts, 2015

BBC Nature has several videos about the Amazon rainforest, river and wildlife:
www.bbc.co.uk/nature/places/Amazon_Basin

15 fantastic rainforest facts from National Geographic Kids:
www.natgeokids.com/uk/discover/geography/physical-geography/15-cool-
things-about-rainforests/

Explore the Rainforest Alliance's site, packed with games and information:
www.rainforest-alliance.org/kids

# INDEX